Greenwillow
Read-alone

# JUDITH S. SEIXAS

# ALLERGIES

## WHAT THEY ARE, WHAT THEY DO

ILLUSTRATED BY
**TOM HUFFMAN**

Greenwillow Books, New York

For Mark and Eli
—J. S. S.

For Michael Nathan
and Adam J.
—T. H.

The artwork was pre-separated by the artist and
printed in two colors. The text type is Plantin.
Text copyright © 1991 by Judith S. Seixas.
Illustrations copyright © 1991 by Tom Huffman.
All rights reserved. No part of this book may be
reproduced or utilized in any form or by any means,
electronic or mechanical, including photocopying,
recording, or by any information storage and
retrieval system, without permission in
writing from the Publisher, Greenwillow Books,
a division of William Morrow & Company, Inc.,
105 Madison Avenue, New York, NY 10016.
Printed in the United States of America
First Edition     10 9 8 7 6 5 4 3 2 1

Library of Congress Cataloging-in-Publication Data

Seixas, Judith S.
Allergies—what they are, what they do /
by Judith S. Seixas; pictures by Tom Huffman.
(A Greenwillow read-alone book)
     p.     cm.
Summary: Outlines various types of allergy symptoms
and describes diagnostic and treatment procedures.
ISBN 0-688-09638-7.     ISBN 0-688-08877-5 (lib  bdg.)
1. Allergy—Juvenile literature.     [1. Allergy.]
I. Title.     RC584.S43     1991
616.97—dc20     90-30753     CIP     AC

335 8248

# CONTENTS

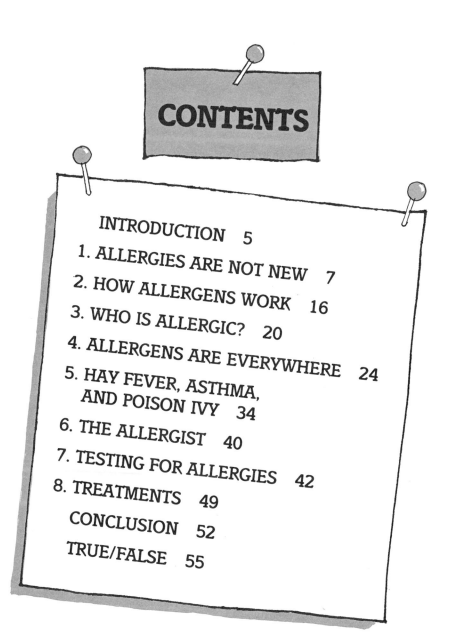

# INTRODUCTION

**A**lmost everyone knows someone
who has an allergy.
More than forty million people
in the United States have allergies.
Perhaps you have a friend
who has to miss school
because she has an asthma attack.

Or you may know somebody
who gets a rash from eating nuts.

Perhaps you have heard
about somebody's mother
who got very sick
after being stung by a bee.

All these people have allergies.
What is an allergy?
An allergy is an unusual reaction
by the body to something
that is harmless for most people.

# « 1 »

# ALLERGIES ARE NOT NEW

## The Records

There are five-thousand-year-old records
from China that tell of people
who had what today
we call allergic reactions.

7

The Chinese believed
that some foods caused sores.
We now think that the people
who had these sores
may have been allergic
to certain foods.

Drawings on the wall
of an ancient king's tomb in Egypt
tell the story of his death
from a bee sting.

Much later, in about 400 B.C.,
Hippocrates, a Greek doctor
who is often called
the father of medicine,
first used the word asthma.
He used it to describe people
who had trouble breathing.
Asthma means "to pant" in Greek.

A second-century Greek doctor named Galen
wrote about people who sneezed when they
came near certain plants.
These plants could well
have been ragweed or grasses.
They are the same plants
that make people
with hay fever sneeze today.

## A Mystery Is Solved

In 1828 an English doctor, John Bostock,

recorded his own symptoms.

He had itchy eyes, a runny nose,

a scratchy throat, and he sneezed.

He knew he did not have a cold.

He thought his symptoms

were due to warm summer weather.

It was not until thirty years later,
in 1852,
that another Englishman,
Dr. W. R. Kirkman,
found the reason
for such symptoms.
In December he gathered
the powdery yellow grains
called pollens
that came from grasses
he grew in his greenhouse.
When he sniffed these pollens,
he began to sneeze.
Then he knew that it was the grass pollens
that made his nose run and itch.
He had discovered the cause of hay fever.

# The First Scratch Test

In the mid-1800's
Charles Blackley,
also an English doctor,
made an important discovery.
He scratched himself
on one arm.
He put a tiny amount
of ryegrass pollen
on the scratch.
The spot itched,
turned red,
and swelled up.

He then scratched his other arm,
but he did not put pollen
on the scratch.
There was no unusual reaction.
He now had proof that his body
reacted to ryegrass pollen.

He had found what came to be known
as the scratch test.
Some doctors still use this test today.

## Allergens and Allergies: How They Were Named

In 1906 an Austrian doctor,

Clemens von Pirquet,

created the word allergen.

He combined two Greek words:

allos, meaning "other,"

and gen, meaning "to produce."

Allergen became the accepted name

for any substance that set off

certain reactions in the body.

Pirquet then made up the word <u>allergy</u>
to describe the body's reaction to allergens.
He combined <u>allos</u> with <u>ergia</u>,
another Greek word meaning "work."

# « 2 »

# HOW ALLERGENS WORK

## Once Is Not Enough

Allergic reactions do not happen
the first time an allergen enters the body.
The body must become sensitive to it.
That happens only after an allergen
has been swallowed, touched,
or breathed in more than once.

## The Body's Mistake

The body's immune system
protects us against harmful invaders,
such as germs and viruses.
It does this by producing "fighters"
called antibodies.
These antibodies destroy the invaders.

In allergic people the immune system
produces a special kind of antibody
against foods or pollens or other substances
that normally are not harmful.
The body reacts by releasing
a chemical called histamine.

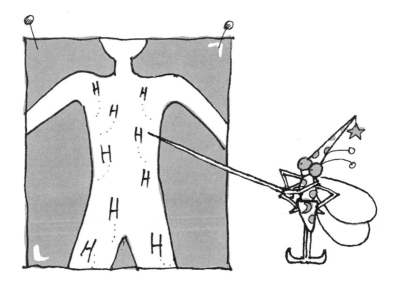

This chemical causes allergic reactions,
such as a runny nose,
wheezing,
or itchy skin.

The most serious
allergic reaction
is called anaphylaxis.
This usually means that it is hard to breathe
or that hives—large, red, itchy bumps—
break out all over the body.

## « 3 »

# WHO IS ALLERGIC?

## Some Questions

It is not known why one person is allergic and another is not. Kay sniffles and sneezes each time she visits her grandparents' farm.

Gus throws up when he eats shellfish.

20

If Rachel is given penicillin
for a sore throat, she gets a rash.

You do not often hear about allergies
to newsprint or poppy seeds.
But some people have these rare allergies.

There are people who have allergies
that come and go or disappear altogether.
No one knows why.
And there are also lucky people
who do not have any allergies.

# Are Allergies Inherited?

Allergies may run in families.

This does not mean that if your parents
have allergies, you will have them.

Often people in the same family
have different allergies.
But if both your parents are allergic,
there is more of a chance
that you will be allergic
than if only one of them
has allergies.

## Let People Know

People who are allergic
should not try to hide
their allergies.
Naomi knew she was
allergic to chocolate.

But she ate some when her friend
asked her to share a candy bar.
Soon she began to itch and feel awful.

Some people wear a tag
listing their allergies.
If one of them
has a serious reaction,
somebody can read the warning
and call for help.

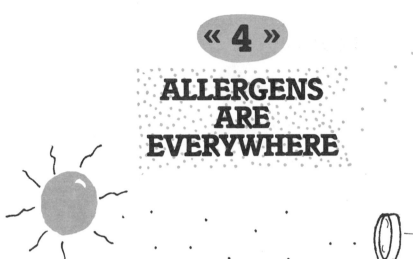

# « 4 »

## ALLERGENS ARE EVERYWHERE

## Allergens in the Air

Allergens in the air usually cannot be seen.

But have you ever looked

at a beam of sunlight?

You can see specks of dust floating in it.

Some of the specks are allergens,

such as mold, dander, and pollen.

Any of these can cause allergic reactions.

## MOLD

Mold is made up of tiny plants.

They usually grow in damp places.

These plants produce spores,

which are very tiny seeds

that blow off into the air.

They can be breathed in easily.

## DANDER

Dander is small scales

from animal hair, skin, and feathers.

Most of the time you cannot see dander.

But we do breathe it in.

## POLLEN

Pollen is the part of a plant
that enables it to breed
and create new plants.
Tree, grass, and weed pollens are powdery.
They are spread by the wind.
Most flower pollens do not cause allergies.
These pollens are heavy and are spread
by bees and hummingbirds
that fly from flower to flower.

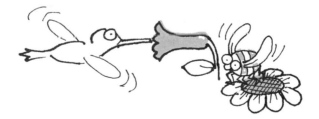

## MITES

Mites are tiny insects.
They are so small
you can breathe them in.
They live in dust.
Therefore, allergies to mites
are often thought
to be allergies to dust.

## Allergens in Food

Allergens in food cause reactions
such as upset stomachs, hives,
or difficulty in breathing.
The foods that most frequently
cause reactions are:
oranges and grapefruits, wheat and corn,
berries, nuts, chocolate, seafood,
eggs, tomatoes, and dairy products.

There are hidden allergens in many foods.
You may not know there is corn
in chewing gum,
baked beans,
and ketchup.
Or you may not know
there is wheat
in hot dogs,
spaghetti,
ice-cream cones,
and many candy bars.

People who are allergic to one food
may be allergic to other foods
in the same food family.
For example, children who are allergic
to milk cannot eat other dairy products,
like ice cream or cheese.

## Allergens in Medicines and Chemicals

Even drugs prescribed by doctors
can sometimes cause allergic reactions,
such as rashes, upset stomachs, swelling,
or shortness of breath.
Aspirin and penicillin
are the most common troublemakers.

The list of chemicals that can cause

skin and breathing problems is a long one.

These chemicals may be found

in paints, soaps, perfumes,

insect sprays, oils, and many more products.

Sometimes people who are not allergic

at first but who work with chemicals

for a long time become allergic to them.

## Allergens in Stings and Insect Bites

Bee or wasp stings are very painful.
But pain does not always mean
an allergic reaction.
A person who is stung on the foot
but gets hives on another part
of the body is allergic.
The bites of fleas, ants,
mosquitoes, and other insects
can also cause allergic reactions.
Most of these are skin reactions,
such as rashes and hives.

## Allergens in Fabrics and Metals

Some people cannot wear wool
or leather next to their skin.
Jewelry made of certain metals
can also cause reactions.

# « 5 »

# HAY FEVER, ASTHMA, AND POISON IVY

## Hay Fever

Hay fever is not caused by hay.

It is not a fever.

It is an allergic reaction

to pollens in the air.

This reaction makes eyes itch,

throats tickle, and people sneeze.

In the northeastern United States ragweed
is the most common cause of hay fever.
In late summer and fall
one ragweed plant can spread
millions of grains of pollen a day.
The pollen is everywhere.
It is even carried by winds over the ocean.

## Asthma

Asthma is usually an allergic reaction
that takes place in the air passages.
It also affects the lungs themselves.

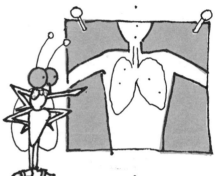

During an asthma attack
it is hard to breathe.
This can be very frightening.
Some children outgrow asthma.
Many do not. Those who do not
must try to stay away
from allergens.

Dusty rooms, old houses, barns, cellars,
attics, and places where people smoke
may bring on attacks.

So may dogs, cats, birds, and rabbits.

If a friend with asthma stays overnight,
he may explain that he can't use
a feather pillow or sleeping bag.
He also may have to stay away
from your pet.

Children with asthma learn the danger signs.
They learn what to do about them.
Sometimes a doctor is needed.
But a child with asthma can lead a healthy
active life most of the time.

TODAY MORE PEOPLE
ARE SUFFERING FROM
ASTHMA BECAUSE OF
AIR POLLUTION.

## Poison Ivy

Poison ivy is a very itchy skin rash.

To get it, all you have to do

is touch the poison ivy plant.

You can also get it from a dog or cat

that has come in contact

with the plant.

It is hard not to scratch the rash.

Some people think scratching

will spread it.

That is not so.

But scratching can cause sores.

Lotions help take the itch away.

If they do not work,

stronger medication

can be prescribed by a doctor.

# THE ALLERGIST

Doctors who search for allergies
and treat them are called allergists.
If a child has an allergy, doctors work
with the parents and the child.
Together they try to identify the allergen.

The doctor asks many questions:

When and where do reactions take place?
What are the symptoms?

Then the doctor decides
what tests are necessary.

# « 7 »

## TESTING FOR ALLERGIES

## You Can Test Yourself

If it is a food that causes the allergy,
people can often test themselves.
For instance, if they suspect eggs,
they can stop eating them,
then see what happens.

| S | M | T | W | T | F | S |
|---|---|---|---|---|---|---|
|   | 1 | 2 | 3 | 4 | 5 | 6 |
| 7 | 8 | 9 | 10 | 11 | 12 | 13 |
| 14 | 15 | 16 | 17 | 18 | 19 | 20 |
| 21 | 22 | 23 | 24 | 25 | 26 | 27 |
| 28 | 29 | 30 |   |   |   |   |

If after a few days
the reaction goes away,
they will know
that eggs caused the trouble.
But if the reaction still continues,
other foods must be tested.
In some cases further testing
by a doctor may be needed.

# How Doctors Test

## SCRATCH TEST

Some doctors use Dr. Blackley's scratch test.
They put a tiny amount of an allergen
on a small scratch.
If there is an allergic reaction,
the scratch becomes red and sore
within a few minutes.

## PATCH TEST

Other doctors use patch tests.
They put a tape that looks
like a Band-Aid on the skin.
It has an allergen on it.
If the person is allergic,
the skin under the tape
will turn red in minutes.

## INTRADERMAL TEST

The test that is used most
is the intradermal skin test.
Intradermal means "under the skin."
The doctor injects allergens
in about eight different spots.
The spots swell and
look like mosquito bites.
If the spot gets sore and red,
the person is allergic
to the allergen injected there.
If the spot itches just a little,
the person is having
a mild reaction.
If nothing happens, the person
is not sensitive to that allergen.

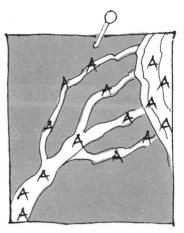

## BLOOD TEST

Antibodies are carried
to the skin
by the blood.
Therefore, the skin and the blood
contain the same antibodies.
Some doctors begin with a blood test.

Most allergists
prefer
skin tests

But most allergists
still prefer skin tests
because there are many allergens
that blood tests cannot detect.

**47**

In blood tests a small amount
of blood is drawn.
Then it is usually sent
to a laboratory.

There the antibodies to suspected
allergens are counted.
If there are large numbers in the blood,
the person being tested is allergic
to that allergen.
When the cause of the problem is found,
the allergy can be treated
with medication or shots.

# « 8 »

# TREATMENTS

## Pills, Sprays, and Nose Drops

In mild reactions, doctors may prescribe an antihistamine. An antihistamine is a drug that can stop the effect of histamine on the body. Antihistamines come in pill or liquid form or nose sprays and drops.

## Allergy Shots

When pills, sprays, and nose drops
do not work, allergic people
can be desensitized.
That means they will no longer
react to the allergen
that has been troubling them.

Here is how it is done:
Each week the doctor
injects some of the allergen
under the skin.

But the doctor never injects
enough to cause a reaction.
Slowly the body gets used
to the allergen.
It takes at least
a few months
for this to happen.

# CONCLUSION

**R**esearchers are working
to find out more about allergies.
Soon there may be new drugs
to prevent allergic reactions
before they begin.
And there may be better drugs
to treat allergies.

Even if you do not have allergies,
you now know how much
people with allergies may suffer.
If you have sisters or brothers
who are allergic, you know
how sick they sometimes feel.
When someone has an allergy,
you will understand his or her problem,
and you may be able
to help friends understand.

If you know what your friends
are allergic to, you can help them
stay away from those allergens.
Most important of all,
if you see someone who is having
a serious allergic reaction,
you know you should get help.

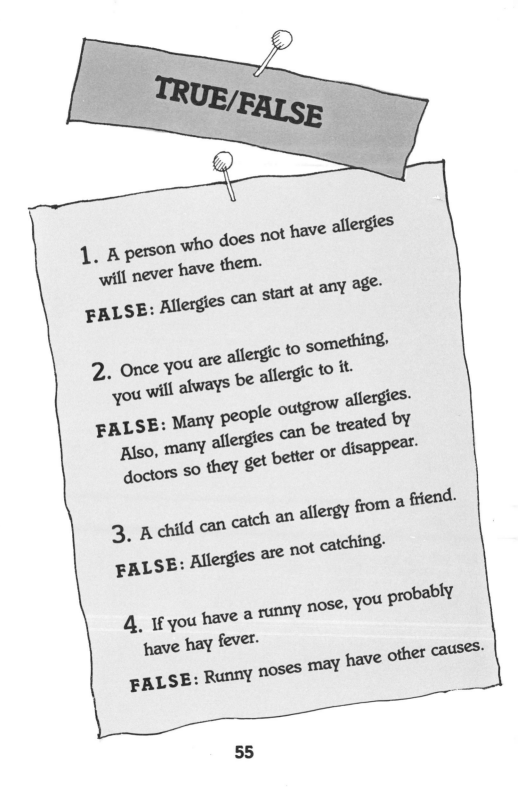

**1.** A person who does not have allergies will never have them.

**FALSE**: Allergies can start at any age.

**2.** Once you are allergic to something, you will always be allergic to it.

**FALSE**: Many people outgrow allergies. Also, many allergies can be treated by doctors so they get better or disappear.

**3.** A child can catch an allergy from a friend.

**FALSE**: Allergies are not catching.

**4.** If you have a runny nose, you probably have hay fever.

**FALSE**: Runny noses may have other causes.

**JUDITH S. SEIXAS** was graduated from Carleton College and has an M.A. from Columbia's Teachers College. She has long been involved in health issues, specializing in the treatment of alcoholics and their families. Her wide experience encompasses both the educational and the therapeutic. She is the co-author of *Children of Alcoholism: A Survivor's Manual*, and for children the author of *Water— What It Is, What It Does*; *Vitamins—What They Are, What They Do*; *Junk Food—What It Is, What It Does*; *Alcohol— What It Is, What It Does*; *Tobacco—What It Is, What It Does*; *Drugs—What They Are, What They Do*; *Living with a Parent Who Drinks Too Much*; and *Living with a Parent Who Takes Drugs.*

**TOM HUFFMAN** attended the School of Visual Arts in New York City and holds a B.A. from the University of Kentucky. Mr. Huffman is a free-lance artist whose works have appeared in galleries, advertisements, and national magazines. He has illustrated many children's books, including nine Greenwillow Read-alone Books.